30 Minutes
... To Brainstorm Great Ideas

GW00514815

Alan Barker

KOGAN PAGE

YOURS TO HAVE AND TO HOLD
BUT NOT TO COPY

First published in 1997
Reprinted 1999

Kogan Page Limited
120 Pentonville Road
London N1 9JN

© Alan Barker, 1997

British Library Cataloguing in Publication Data
A CIP record for this book is available from the British Library.

ISBN 0 7494 2358 7

Typeset by Florencetype Ltd, Stoodleigh, Devon
Printed in England by Clays Ltd, St Ives plc

CONTENTS

Introduction   **5**

1 What is Brainstorming?   **7**
Alex Osborn's four rules of brainstorming 8;
Thinking outside ourselves 9; The two stages of
thinking 10; Associative thinking 13; Why most
brainstorming isn't 16

2 Planning the Session   **20**
Assembling the team 20; Defining the task 23;
Task as Given 27; Drawing up a timetable 28;
Points of procedure 30; Venue and equipment 31

3 Exploring the Problem   **33**
Creative listening 34; 'How to' 36; Task as
Understood 38

4 Generating Ideas   **40**
'How about . . .' 40; Using an oracle 42;
Metaphorical thinking 43; Reversal techniques 47;
Selecting ideas 50

5 Developing the Solution   **55**
Evaluating the solution 57; Stakeholders and
sponsors 58; Mapping out a plan of action 63;
Taking the first step 64

The 30 Minutes Series

The Kogan Page 30 Minutes Series has been devised to give your confidence a boost when faced with tackling a new skill or challenge for the first time.

So the next time you're thrown in at the deep end and want to bring your skills up to scratch or pep up your career prospects, turn to the *30 Minutes Series* for help!

Titles available are:

30 Minutes Before Your Job Interview

30 Minutes Before a Meeting

30 Minutes Before a Presentation

30 Minutes to Boost Your Communication Skills

30 Minutes to Brainstorm Great Ideas

30 Minutes to Deal with Difficult People

30 Minutes to Succeed in Business Writing

30 Minutes to Master the Internet

30 Minutes to Make the Right Decision

30 Minutes to Make the Right Impression

30 Minutes to Plan a Project

30 Minutes to Prepare a Job Application

30 Minutes to Write a Business Plan

30 Minutes to Write a Marketing Plan

30 Minutes to Write a Report

30 Minutes to Write Sales Letters

Available from all good booksellers.
For further information on the series, please contact:

Kogan Page, 120 Pentonville Road, London N1 9JN
Tel: 0171 278 0433 Fax: 0171 837 6348

INTRODUCTION

We are paid to think. Our success depends on our results, and we think when we want results that are better than they would be without thinking. Yet we rarely think about the way we think, or see it as a skill that we might develop. Few of us are trained to think. Brainstorming helps us think more clearly and creatively.

At the heart of the process is a distinction between two types of thinking: having ideas, and making use of them. Many of our conversations are messy mixtures of the two: our first reaction to an idea tends to be to judge, evaluate or criticize it. As a result, neither kind of thinking is entirely successful. The most important skill in brainstorming is separating these two types of thinking, and keeping them separate.

Brainstorming cheerfully demolishes a number of myths about thinking.

■ Thinking is not intelligence: some of the best ideas in a brainstorming session are the least intelligent

- You don't have to be educated well to think well: highly educated people are not necessarily good thinkers and good ideas can come from the least expert or experienced in the group

- Thinking is not hoarding information: the less information we have in a brainstorm, the freer our thinking will be

- Thinking doesn't have to be logical: brainstorming thrives on wild, irrational connections between ideas.

This book explains how to conduct a formal group brainstorming session. But you can use nearly all the techniques described here, by themselves, either alone or in a meeting. Similarly, you could conduct any part of the brainstorm process in isolation, or space the sections over several days to give people time to think further.

Above all, brainstorming provides practical proof that thinking can be fun!

1

WHAT IS BRAINSTORMING?

Brainstorming is a structured process for having ideas.

It was invented in the late 1930s by an American advertising executive, Alex Osborn. He was convinced that success in any enterprise demands a creative approach: 'Imagination', he wrote, 'is the cornerstone of human endeavour.' He also noticed that, particularly in meetings, new ideas were discouraged or destroyed by consistent kinds of behaviour – especially if the ideas were weak (as new ideas often are), or offered by someone of low rank. He became determined to find a way to counter these behaviours and release people's creativity.

The process he developed operates according to a few simple principles. When a meeting followed the rules, Osborn discovered that people generated dozens of ideas very quickly – many of them new and a few extremely valuable. Brainstorming so obviously improved the output of meetings that it soon became a marketable and extremely popular idea.

Alex Osborn's four rules of brainstorming

1. *Criticism is ruled out*: adverse judgement of ideas must be withheld until later.

2. *'Freewheeling' is welcomed*: the wilder the idea, the better; it is easier to tame down than to think up.

3. *Quantity is wanted*: the greater the number of ideas, the more the likelihood of winners.

4. *Combination and improvement are sought*: in addition to contributing ideas of their own, participants should suggest how ideas of others can be turned into better ideas; or how two or more ideas can be joined into still another idea.

(Applied Imagination, 1953)

Osborn doesn't develop the rules of brainstorming much further. He emphasizes the importance of:

■ Getting going – not waiting for inspiration to strike
■ Focus – on the task in hand
■ Attention – of the whole group to one kind of thinking at a time
■ Concentration – sticking at it, refusing to give up if no ideas come.

Above all, he stresses effort. Again and again, he insists that nothing is more vital to the session's success than working hard.

Brainstorming has prospered and developed in many ways. It has become a component of learning organizations, scenario planning, teambuilding, performance management and the whole quality movement. It has spawned many new techniques and found echoes in the work of thinkers like Edward de Bono and Roger van Oech.

Synectics, in particular, has contributed enormously to brainstorming. During the 1960s, WJ Gordon and George Prince combined new ways of thinking creatively with inter-personal skills to help people think together more effi-ciently and productively. Synectics contributes a detailed structure to the brainstorming session, provides new and powerful thinking techniques and suggests how the group can behave to stimulate creativity.

Thinking outside ourselves

Osborn apparently took inspiration for brainstorming from an ancient Hindu technique called Prai-Barshana, meaning 'questioning outside yourself'.

If we haven't an idea in our head, we often say we're 'stuck'. The word is apt. We are locked into the mental pat-terns that govern our everyday thinking. Osborn, indeed, called this state 'functional fixation'; more recently, we have come to call these patterns 'mindsets' or 'paradigms'.

Mindsets are an inevitable part of thinking. They create the assumptions without which thinking is impossible. Mindsets are useful: they help us get things done. They let us down, however, when we want to find new ideas, because they dictate the way we find them and define the ideas themselves. So finding new ideas means stepping outside, or 'breaking', the mindset. 'Problems', wrote Albert Einstein, 'cannot be solved by thinking within the frame-work in which the problems were created.'

Because mindsets are so strong, we must deliberately think our way beyond them. Brainstorming is designed to do just that: it helps us 'think outside ourselves'.

The two cycles

Most of our work is located in a cycle of operational think-ing: acting, evaluating the effects of our actions, thinking about improving or changing what are doing and planning new actions. Operational thinking involves routines, procedures, rules and known solutions.

If we want to find new ideas, we must move out of this cycle into the creative thinking cycle. In this cycle, we think in a radically different way: exploring, discovering, developing ideas and validating or checking them. We can then bring our discoveries back into the operational cycle as practical solutions.

There are only two reasons for crossing from the operational to the creative cycle:

- we have to – a crisis; a known solution fails
- we choose to – we make a deliberate decision to explore.

Brainstorming is a way of making the move from operational thinking into creative thinking. Everybody in the session must understand that we are in the creative cycle, and that operational thinking is not appropriate (see Figure 1).

The two stages of thinking

Osborn called brainstorming 'organized ideation'. He contrasts ideation (generating ideas) with judgement (sifting through the ideas, choosing, categorizing or rejecting). One of the central ideas of brainstorming is 'suspended judgement': separating judgement from ideation and postponing it.

We can imagine thinking as a process in two stages. First-stage thinking (what Osborn called 'ideation') is perception: we recognize something because it fits some pre-existing mental pattern. We can call these mental patterns 'ideas'. Ideas allow us to make sense of our experiences; they are the means by which we have experiences.

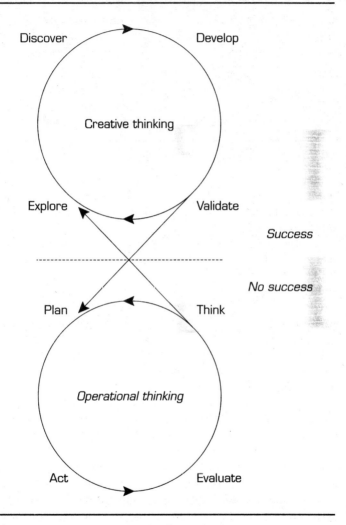

Figure 1 *The two cycles of thinking*

First stage	Second stage
Perception: sensation intuition	Judgement: reason evaluation

Reality >>   >> *Language* >>   >> *Action*

What can we see? What might it be?	What does it mean? How do we judge it?

Figure 2 *The two stages of thinking*

Recognizing something allows us to name it. First-stage thinking turns experience into language: words, pictures, computer code or whatever.

We perceive using our senses and our intuition. Our senses tell us that something is there; our intuition tells us about its potential: what it might contain, where it might have come from, how it might develop.

In second-stage thinking (Osborn's 'judgement'), we manipulate language in order to do something useful. We judge using reason and evaluation. Reason gives meaning to what we have perceived; evaluation tells us whether we like it or not, and what we might choose to do about it (see Figure 2).

We are much better at second-stage than at first-stage thinking. We are taught to reason and evaluate at school: we can even build computers to do second-stage thinking for us. We are so good at second-stage thinking that we often think that it's the only kind of thinking. We often ignore the first stage completely, and take our perceptions for granted. This leaping to judgement is what Osborn warns us against: it is the sworn enemy of brainstorming.

Brainstorming is a way of developing first-stage thinking skills. Having an idea is a matter of seeing reality differently.

Associative thinking

A brainstorming session is a journey of discovery. We find new ideas by exploring: by taking an excursion away from operational thinking, from the known world of regulations, routine and working solutions, into an uncharted land of possibilities and intrigue. We can imagine new ideas as buried treasure, waiting to be discovered. 'Creativity', wrote Joseph Campbell, 'is going out to find the thing society hasn't found yet.'

This journey of discovery demands a special kind of thinking. The more freedom of movement we allow ourselves in our first-stage thinking, the greater the chances of finding something really new (see Figure 3).

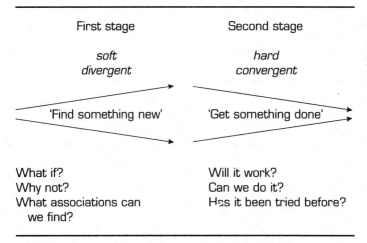

Figure 3 *The two stages of creative thinking*

13

The first stage involves divergent thinking: widening our perceptions by questioning assumptions, by looking at material in new ways or by making random juxtapositions with unrelated ideas. Our purpose is to find something new.

The second stage uses convergent thinking: judging the ideas we have found and developing them as something of use by using logic, sorting, measurement and analysis, comparison against objectives. Our purpose is to get something done.

Of course, exploring in unknown regions can be scary. There may be no map to guide us; no pioneers who can tell us where the reefs and crevasses are. Creative thinking is always risky. Brainstorming helps us to manage the risk.

Fortunately help is at hand in the shape of associative thinking. We think associatively whenever we make links between ideas to make new ideas. We all have a natural ability to think associatively. We wouldn't be able to learn or remember anything without it. On the whole, however, our talent for associative thinking is not nurtured, at school or at work.

Associative thinking is at the heart of brainstorming. The more we can make connections between ideas, the more new ideas we will find. The more unlikely or surprising the connection, the more creative the new idea will be. 'Creativity', to quote Thomas Disch, 'is the ability to see relationships where none exist.'

Associative thinking is identical to Edward de Bono's famous 'lateral thinking', which he contrasts with 'vertical thinking'. In vertical thinking, we have to be correct at every stage in order to have a final correct answer. In lateral thinking, we don't have to be right at any stage, because we aren't seeking a correct answer. 'The purpose of lateral thinking', writes de Bono, 'is movement – from one concept to another, from one way of looking at things to another.'

When we think associatively, we use ideas as stepping stones – and the important thing is to keep moving.

Making connections

Generate four numbers randomly. You could do this by throwing dice. If none are to hand, try using today's date or the number of your house or flat. As a quick creative game, try to think of other ways of generating random numbers!

Use the first three digits to locate a page in a big dictionary. Use the fourth digit to locate a single word. If you don't have a dictionary, use any book, newspaper or magazine you can find, using the numbers somehow to locate a page and a word. If the word you have found is a concrete noun – something that exists physically – write it on a piece of paper. If it is not, find the first concrete noun following.

Now spend 30 seconds writing down all the words that spring into your mind when you look at the 'trigger word'. It doesn't matter why or how you arrive at them; the object is to capture as many as possible.

You may find it easier to use images rather than words. Use the numbers to find a picture in a magazine or book. Let other pictures come into your mind. Note down what your imagination sees. Maybe you can make more connections using other imaginary senses: touch, smell, taste, sound. The trick is to let your mind wander and capture what you find!

You can use other sources of information. Look out of the window and identify the third object with any green in it. Use random numbers to locate a company in the stock market figures and ask what they make. A friend of mine opens her Koran at random and meditates on the first sentence she reads.

Playing this game uses your powers of associative thinking. Your ability to make 'lateral leaps' from word to word, or from picture to picture, will be enormously useful during the brainstorming session.

Why most brainstorming isn't

Brainstorming has acquired something of a mixed reputation. No other thinking technique has become so familiar. The word has entered the dictionaries and is regularly used to describe any kind of 'free-form thinking'. Yet it is often misunderstood, and most brainstorming sessions are actually nothing of the kind. As a result, many people have come to see brainstorming as useless, self-indulgent or a waste of time.

There are three broad reasons why most brainstorming isn't:

- The session tries to tackle the wrong kind of problem
- Group behaviour gets in the way
- The session is unstructured.

The wrong kind of problem

The only good reason to hold a brainstorming session is to generate new ideas. And only some kinds of problem need to be tackled by generating ideas.

Brainstorming is not the way to handle a crisis. Necessity may be the mother of invention, but a crisis needs rapid decisions and clear leadership. If a person – or a company – is bleeding to death, our first priority is saving the patient. Asking how we can stop the same accident recurring will have to wait until later.

Brainstorming is not appropriate if something needs to be put right. If we know what's wrong, and we know clearly what it will look like when it's put right, we need to organize an effective repair job. Many technical, mechanical and administrative problems are of this kind. If it's broke, fix it.

Brainstorming is unnecessary when you want to work out a plan. If you know where you are, and precisely where you want to be at a definite point in the future, start planning. Of course, the future is uncertain and you will almost certainly need to revise your plan; but that's no reason not to have a plan in the first place.

All these three types of problem are operational and require operational solutions.

Brainstorming is the appropriate way to tackle problems that are not operational: challenges that are open-ended, fuzzy or broadly conceived. When we genuinely want to think in terms of possibilities, brainstorming is the tool we need.

People behaving badly

In all too many brainstorms, people's behaviour actually stops them generating ideas.

Inhibiting behaviour is usually the result of operational thinking. It is essential that everybody in the group understands that responses 'in operational mode' are unhelpful, except in specific parts of the session. Some kinds of operational thinking are so common that it's worth mentioning them. Because we are so accustomed to them, we may not even notice that they are happening.

We are accustomed to focus on results. If we focus on solutions rather than possibilities, we will generate very few ideas, and even fewer genuinely new ones. Focusing on results means that we judge an idea by its usefulness or feasibility, rather than its novelty or potential. A new idea will probably not be a good one until we develop it;

17

focusing on results will lead us to kill off the idea before it has a chance to grow.

We find it difficult not to judge ideas. We are taught from an early age to argue and to be critical. Ask anybody what they think about something: almost inevitably they will begin by finding fault with it. One of the central disciplines of brainstorming is to forbid any evaluative remarks during first-stage thinking. Watch out for comments such as:

- 'That doesn't make sense.'
- 'It won't work.'
- 'We tried that before and it failed.'
- 'We haven't the money.'
- 'Totally impractical.'
- 'Too complicated.'
- 'You'll never get people to change.'

Evaluation must be rigorously postponed until the group goes into second-stage thinking.

Politics can stop people offering ideas. One of the most common reasons for brainstorming failing is the 'political' behaviour in the group. Ideas are as powerful as the people expressing them. High status people can give ideas great weight simply by suggesting or supporting them. They can kill an idea stone dead by a mere shrug. Others can be intimidated by the presence of superiors or seniors: they may clam up, defer to authority, or offer only politically acceptable ideas. If we are brainstorming because we've been ordered to, we may limit our thinking to those ideas that will advance our careers. If we haven't been adequately briefed, and are unclear what the session's objective is, we may start to suspect hidden agendas.

Lack of attention to process

The idea that brainstorming is 'free-form' or extempore has done as much harm as good. Very few interesting ideas will be generated in a session that lacks structure or discipline.

Brainstorming is a kind of game and, like any game, it needs agreed rules and regulations to be successful and enjoyable. These conventions include a carefully selected team, a clear task and a structured timetable. Good preparation is essential if we want the session to have a chance of success.

2

PLANNING THE SESSION

Planning the session means thinking about 'the three Ts':

- Team
- Task
- Timetable.

There are no guarantees that your session will be successful. Brainstorming is a pragmatic and intuitive process – your skills will improve most by running sessions and carefully reviewing them. But clarifying these three key issues before you begin will give you a head start.

Assembling the team

The best number for a brainstorming team is between eight and 12. Osborn advocates a mix of 'core members' and 'guests' in roughly equal proportions; the 'core members' are more experienced in brainstorming and act as pacesetters. The team should be a 'rich mix'. Include representatives from as many different functions, departments or specialisms as possible. A team made up of representatives from different organizations can be particularly effective – though difficult to organize.

As well as a functional 'rich mix', the team should ideally include as many managerial levels as possible. Pragmatically, however, we must recognize the potential problems of including too many ranks. Senior managers can easily take over the session; very junior staff may feel uncomfortable, frustrated or patronized. It may be better to avoid too wide a spread and include only people of similar rank.

The team should break down into three clearly defined roles.

Chair

The Chair is in command of the session's process and procedures. So, being a facilitator, they must understand the process well. The Chair's roles are to:

- Manage the session: signal the start and end of each section and focus on the techniques appropriate to each
- Stop people talking at once
- Encourage people who are not contributing
- Prohibit evaluation (except during second-stage thinking)
- Check that everybody is taking notes of ideas
- Review ideas when they dry up
- Keep time.

You might consider employing an external facilitator, who can challenge organizational mindsets and internal politics more effectively.

21

The Chair should not be the 'owner' of the task or problem. That responsibility belongs to the client.

Client

This should be somebody other than the Chair. Clear individual ownership of the task means that the task can be more clearly defined at the start; the team is more motivated to tackle the problem and satisfy the client; ideas can be more realistically judged and developed; somebody will take responsibility for implementing the solution.

The client may be a member of the brainstorming team or – a more satisfactory arrangement – a guest from outside.

Thinkers

The rest of the team act as 'creative consultants': a resource placed at the service of the client and managed by the Chair. Their roles are to treat the client as a valued customer, listen, generate ideas, offer suggestions, generate solutions and give opinions only when asked for.

You may wish to include people on the basis of their competences and create a balanced mix of:

- Ideas people (who are good at 'planting' ideas or cross-fertilizing from elsewhere)
- Actioners (skilled in planning, directing, turning ideas into working propositions)
- Administrators (who analyse well, check details and build practicability)
- Carers (who build communication in the team and maximize the potential of others)

In particular, you may wish to include a few 'self-starters', whose natural talent for having ideas can get things moving; but be careful not to let them dominate the session.

Beware of inviting too many experts. The very last thing a brainstorming session needs is specialized knowledge or experience of the matter being considered. If anything, the team should contain more 'innocents', whose relative ignorance makes them more open-minded.

Defining the task

Brainstorming works best when the problem is 'owned' by the client, and is appropriate for the process. Clarifying these two points before the session will help to make the session a success – and will save time.

Who owns the problem?

Problems without owners tend to become problems without solutions. First, then, identify your client. Before the session, the Chair should confirm with them that they:

- Have responsibility for the problem
- Are accountable for the solution
- Honestly want to solve it
- Have the power to do something about it
- Don't already have an answer
- Are genuinely open to new suggestions.

It's essential that the client is truly committed to finding a solution: so committed that they're willing to consider any possibilities. What matters is their passion – the sense of urgency or necessity that drives them to seek a new approach.

Presented or constructed?

The task should be in a form suitable for brainstorming. It should be the 'right kind of problem'.

We can categorize problems broadly as presented and constructed. Presented problems happen to us. We have had no control over them, and are not responsible for them. Presented problems prevent us getting where we want to go: they are obstacles in our path. Examples include:

- The photocopier breaking down
- A competitor's new product invading our market
- New legislation or regulations affecting our operations
- Having to work with 'difficult' people.

Constructed problems, by contrast, are challenges that we set ourselves. The problem didn't exist before we created it. There may not be anything specifically wrong; we are interested in possibilities: of improvement, or change, or something different.

Examples include:

- Gaining a qualification
- Improving our performance
- Innovating a new product
- Increasing market share
- Working out a long-term strategy.

Brainstorming works best with constructed problems. The easiest and quickest way to construct one is to cast it as a 'How to' statement. This:

- Gives us responsibility for the task
- Expresses the task in forward-looking terms (rather than in terms of putting right a past error or finding a cause)
- Suggests multiple possibilities.

'How to': transforming a problem

The 'How to' technique can transform even the most stressful presented problem. Look at what happens when we recast the examples we gave earlier:

- The photocopier breaking down
  How to mend the photocopier
  How to get the photocopier mended
  How to stop the photocopier breaking down
  How to make copies without using the photocopier

- A competitor's new product invading our market
  How to deal with the invasion
  How to stop the invasion
  How to defend our market
  How to find a new market

- New legislation or regulations affecting our operations
  How to conform
  How to change the way we operate
  How to use the new rules to our advantage
  How to avoid being affected by the new rules

- Having to work with 'difficult' people
  How to work around them
  How to make them less difficult
  How to make life a little easier for ourselves
  How to understand them

In each case, the effect of 'How to' is to open up the problem by creating a number of action-centred possibilities, by thinking forward and – above all – by giving us responsibility for the task. We are 'unstuck'.

Loosening the structure of the problem

We can further categorize problems in terms of their structure: as well-structured or ill-structured. We can evaluate a problem's structure in terms of its:

- Initial conditions (where we are)
- Goal conditions (where we want to be)
- Operators (the means or methods of moving from initial to goal conditions).

A well-structured problem (WSP) has clear initial conditions, goal conditions and operators. An ill-structured problem (ISP) is unclear in any or all of these respects.

'How to mend the photocopier' is a well-structured problem – if we are expert in mending photocopiers. The initial conditions are clear (the machine isn't working); goal conditions are clear (we can easily see when it is working); and operators are clear (we have a set of specific procedures to isolate the problem and put it right). Of course, lack of expertise will make the operators less clear, and the problem more ill-structured – and stressful.

Many constructed problems are best handled by structuring them well. Gaining a qualification depends on a clear timetable and explicit study guidelines. Completing a project on time and to budget means planning the operators carefully and reviewing them regularly.

Brainstorming, on the other hand, works best with ill-structured problems. We may be uncertain of our present situation; we may have no precise idea of our goal, or of how to achieve it. The problem may be ill-structured because:

- It has no cause
- It has many causes
- We can't remove the cause or causes

- We don't have enough information to go on
- We have too much information to see the problem clearly
- The information is ambiguous
- We have no precedent to follow
- The precedent is inadequate as a guide to success
- The variables are difficult to measure
- Time is limited
- We want to do something different.

If the problem is ill-structured, brainstorming may be the best way to tackle it. Put another way, if we want to brainstorm the problem, we must make it as ill-structured as possible.

Task as Given

Invite the client, before the session, to prepare a short presentation of the task as they see it. This should last no more than five minutes. Ask them to explain the problem in as concrete and personal a way as they can.

They could use this list of questions as triggers to help them. They should be ready to begin by 'headlining' their chosen 'How to'.

How to

Background: how has the task come about? Why does it need to be done? What is the context?

Ownership: why are you involved? Where does it hurt? How does it affect you personally? What is motivating you to find a solution?

Past efforts: what's already been tried or considered? By whom? Do any solutions already exist? Why are they unsatisfactory?

Power to act: what are you in a position to do? What are you willing to do? What constraints are you operating within? Who else is involved? In what way?

Ideal solution: a big wish. If miracles could happen, what would you ask for? What is your vision of the future? Wish for the impossible!

The client might conclude their presentation by using statements such as:

- 'What I'd really like to do or see happen is . . . '

- 'If I could break all the rules of reality, I would . . . ' – and they could end by 'underlining' the Task as Given 'The main point is . . . '

Drawing up a timetable

Most brainstorming sessions are too long. Thirty minutes is ideal; 45 minutes is probably an outside limit. Energy levels will stay high in a short session. Generating ideas is intense, emotionally exhausting work, and there is nothing worse than a session collapsing into silence while people desperately try to think up something new to offer.

From the beginning, Alex Osborn divided brainstorming into two sections, ideation and judgement. Synectics (and other creative approaches) add another section, in which the team explores the problem itself and decides – with the client – on its goal.

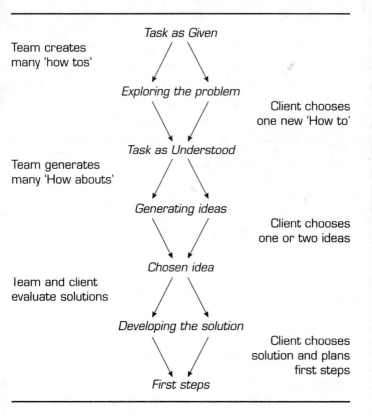

Figure 4 *Three sections of the brainstorming session*

The session now divides neatly into three sections.

1. *Exploring the problem*: the client proposes the 'Task as Given', and the team discusses and reformulates it as a 'Task as Understood'.

2. *Generating ideas*: the team generates ideas for tackling the 'Task as Understood', in the form of 'How about's. The client selects one promising idea for development.

3. *Developing the solution*: team and client together assess the strengths and weaknesses of promising ideas and develop an idea into a feasible proposal.

Each section uses both stages of creative thinking. The first stage involves 'opening up' or divergent thinking: postponing judgement, challenging mindsets, accumulating a range of possibilities. The second stage involves 'closing down' or convergent thinking: selecting, focusing, and developing material into something useful (see Figure 4).

Points of procedure

The success of the session will depend as much on your intuition and sensitivity as on careful planning. You may wish to consider some additional suggestions for improving or varying the way you run the session.

Setting targets

The team may work better if you set deadlines and targets. The discipline of 'scoring' can produce more ideas, and help crazier ideas to surface. People may also enjoy an atmosphere of playful rivalry, splitting into subgroups and competing to beat each other on numbers of ideas. Setting targets is something you must judge with practice. A 30-minute brainstorming session, divided equally into three sections of 10 minutes, can produce between 50 and 100 ideas per section.

Varying the structure

You may wish to vary the format of the session. You could do this by:

- Briefing the team with the client's task prior to the session, to allow for private musing and 'sleeping on the problem'

- Beginning the session with a 'warm-up' exercise, unrelated to the task in hand

- Taking breaks between sections, so that people can 'walk away' from their thinking – and allow their intuition to add further ideas

- Holding separate sessions for each section, particularly for solution development

- Inviting further written contributions for any section after the session.

Separating individual and group brainstorming

An idea is only ever the product of a single mind. Solitary thinking is best for having ideas; group thinking is best for building on them. Brainstorming should use both.

Consider using individual brainstorming to begin generating ideas. If you make it clear that all ideas will be gathered anonymously, people are less likely to censor their own ideas or to limit their thinking.

Group brainstorming can then use this material to generate more ideas – by doing what groups do best: triggering or 'sparking' ideas off other ideas, combining, developing, improving or varying them.

Venue and equipment

The environment and equipment for the session will strongly influence its outcome. The office will tend to reinforce the office mindset. Consider using a new location, perhaps completely away from the workplace. The room you use should be:

- Large enough to accommodate the team, with maybe small tables for breakaway groups
- Comfortable
- Well-ventilated and lit
- Suitable for displaying plenty of flipchart sheets or newsprint
- Private – no telephone (and ask people to switch off their mobiles).

Other essential equipment will probably include:

- Flipcharts (preferably more than one) and a large stock of pads
- Marker pens
- Notepads and pencils
- Masking tape and/or Blu-tack
- Post-it notes or cards for recording and rearranging ideas.

In addition, you could provide:

- A large dictionary or dictionaries
- A pile of books and magazines
- A pair of dice (for generating random numbers)
- Some of the lists of ideas suggested in Chapter 4.

All of these can come in handy as resources during the session.

3

EXPLORING
THE PROBLEM

A problem well understood is half solved. The purpose of the session's first stage, then, is to explore the problem as fully as possible (see Figure 5). The team's goal is:

■ To find the part or form of the problem most suitable for creative treatment

■ First-stage thinking: the team listens to the Task as Given, finding new ways of looking at it, creating new expressions of it

■ Second-stage thinking: the client chooses a new form of the task – the Task as Understood. The team judges its suitability for creative thinking and takes it forward to the session's next section.

The Chair opens the session by inviting the client to present the task. The team listens to the 'Task as Given' in order to construct new versions of it. The client's presentation will work best if they:

- Are given the chance to prepare it before the session
- Have only a limited amount of time to present
- Express the problem as concretely or evocatively as possible.

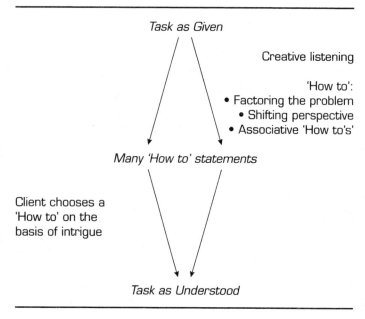

Figure 5 *How the problem is explored*

Creative listening

The team's first job is to listen as closely as possible while the client presents the Task as Given.

A typical speaking rate is 150–200 words per minute; the mind, however, can process words at 800–1000 wpm. We can have lots of thoughts and ideas while someone is speaking to us. As a result, we hold two conversations: external and internal. Very often, we may find ourselves listening more to our internal conversation than to the external one. We usually call this 'daydreaming' and regard it as 'wrong'. In fact, when the mind wanders it may find interesting new ideas. The trick is to be able to capture them so that we can use them.

In/out listening allows us to listen to the internal conversation and record whatever it tells us. We can then return to the external conversation with renewed attention. It also stops us forgetting what we wanted to say, and can stop us interrupting.

Some of our internal ideas will be triggered by the client's presentation. They may include:

- Key words that sum up some aspect of the problem
- Examples offered by the client
- Examples from elsewhere that occur to us
- Similarities with other parts of our experience
- Analogies, images or metaphors that spring to mind
- Ideas for solutions
- Judgements about what the client is saying
- Something you want to say or ask.

Other ideas will seem quite irrelevant: they may relate to what is worrying us at the time, dreams, desires or worries. Often the thoughts may be silly, outrageous, rude, 'politically incorrect' or immoral. Try to avoid self-censorship. The idea is private; you don't have to share it. Once you've noted it, put it out of your head and go back to listening.

'How to'

Once the client has presented the Task as Given, the team uses the notes they've made to create new 'How to's. These are best written on Post-it notes, one 'How to' per note, and displayed on a table or wall for sorting.

The team's new 'How to's may take many forms:

- An alternative definition of the task
- A challenge
- A wish
- A goal
- An embryonic idea
- An image.

Virtually anything is acceptable, as long as it addresses the client's task respectfully and constructively. Remember that our role is to help!

You might suggest individual brainstorming first: people record their ideas alone and submit them anonymously. If you have time, the team (or subgroups) could then use this material to trigger new 'How to's by combining, transforming or improving them.

Factoring the problem

Can you break the Task as Given into parts? Each then can become a new 'How to'. What has the client's presentation suggested about the various elements of the task? Look for:

- Contributing factors
- Consequences or knock-on effects
- Functional aspects (design, production, financial, personnel, administrative . . .)

- Different points of view on the task
- Departments or teams affected
- Time factors (short term, long term)
- Geographical factors (global, local, sectors).

Some of these are problems that the client might tackle straight away: operational issues, technical or mechanistic problems that present no immediate difficulty – although the client may not have thought of them. Others may require further brainstorming.

Shifting perspective

Taking the Task as Given, we can shift our perspective on it to create new expressions of it. We can go in two directions:

- 'Forwards', by asking 'What do we need to do to achieve the task?'
- 'Backwards', by asking 'If we could achieve the task, what problem would it solve?'

Forward shifting will tend to generate more specific 'How to's', which are probably best tackled as planning problems. Backward shifts will generate more general 'How to's', which may be more suitable for creative treatment.

Associative 'How to's'

We can use any of the words, ideas, or images from our internal conversation to generate new 'How to's'. Perhaps a word suggests some metaphor for the problem, or a character from a story who tackled a similar problem in an interesting way. The word may suggest another that sounds similar. We might take one of our notes and make a list of 10 or 20 words by spontaneous association. Each word then becomes a trigger for a new idea.

The most interesting 'How to's' can emerge from the most unlikely connections. Go for the words or images that seem furthest from the Task as Given: those with least apparent relevance. These have the most potential for novel ideas.

Task as Understood

Before long, the client will be faced with a large number of new 'How to's', many of which may be of interest in some way. They must now choose one to take forward to the second part of the session as the Task as Understood. A team working well for five minutes might produce anything up to 150 ideas. Sorting and choosing can be a bewildering prospect.

Ask the client to sort the 'How to's' into three broad categories:

1. Realistic ideas that could be actioned immediately. They may be known solutions or fallback solutions that you could put to one side

2. Embryonic ideas that could become realistic solutions after modification or development. Useful as starting points for thinking at a later stage

3. Intriguing ideas. An intriguing idea excites us: we can't see where it leads; we may not understand it entirely; it may scare us. But we are drawn to it and feel compelled to explore further. Perhaps it expresses the very essence of the problem. Maybe it makes us laugh or say: 'Wow! If we could do that, all our problems will be solved.'

The most intriguing idea often leaps out at us suddenly. But it's important to give the client enough time to become intrigued.

Once the client has chosen the Task as Understood, we should allow them to say, briefly, why it intrigues them. We should also check that it is ill-structured enough to be suitable for creative treatment.

- Are the initial conditions too clear?
- Are goal conditions too clear?
- Are the operators too clear?

Remember that all the other 'How to's' are material with the potential for 'recycling' later. The brainstorming session has begun to produce useful results even at this early stage.

4

GENERATING IDEAS

The second stage of the session takes us furthest on our creative excursion (see Figure 6). Its purpose is:

■ To find ideas for possible solutions that we can present to the client

■ First-stage thinking: the team explores and finds ideas for tackling the Task as Understood. These are best expressed as 'How about's'.

■ Second-stage thinking: the team chooses some of the ideas and develops them as potential solutions – not in great detail, but enough to convince the client that they are feasible.

'How about . . . '

Generating ideas should be fun. This part of the session can provoke wild ideas and stormy laughter. Encourage

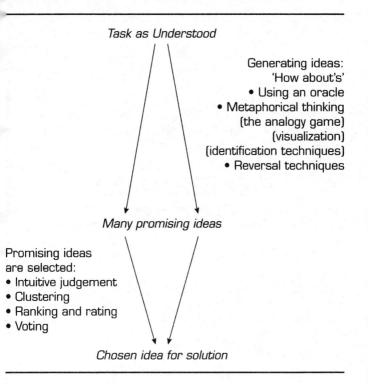

Task as Understood

Generating ideas:
'How about's'
• Using an oracle
• Metaphorical thinking
(the analogy game)
(visualization)
(identification techniques)
• Reversal techniques

Many promising ideas

Promising ideas
are selected:
• Intuitive judgement
• Clustering
• Ranking and rating
• Voting

Chosen idea for solution

Figure 6 *How ideas are generated*

craziness and flights of fancy, but ensure that people concentrate on creating 'How about's': possible courses of action to tackle the Task as Understood. Ask them to record their thoughts – especially the silliest ones. Do everything you can to keep the team's thinking moving.

It can be useful to set targets: time limits and quotas of ideas, both at the first stage (to generate as many as

41

possible), and at the second (when the team presents potential solutions to the client). You may want to experiment with breaking the team into smaller syndicates and introduce an element of playful competition.

You may decide to invite the client to 'sit out' during this part of the session. It can be very dangerous to allow them to participate: they may, with the best of intentions, stifle the team with operational thinking: 'That would never work', 'We've tried that', 'You must be joking' and so on. They may also slow down the proceedings by discussing ideas in detail.

There are hundreds of ways in which we can generate 'How about's'. I've gathered together some of the most powerful and enjoyable: those that have worked best in the sessions I've seen or facilitated. I've 'graded' the techniques very roughly in order of difficulty: some seem to generate large numbers of ideas more quickly than others, depending on the experience and taste of the team. Don't feel that you need to use all of them! Try them out in different sessions; invent your own variations.

Using an oracle

In many cultures, someone wanting to find a new way of looking at a problem would consult an oracle. The most famous is probably Apollo's oracle at Delphi; others include the Tarot, the runes and the ancient Chinese book of divination, the *I Ching*. These oracles are designed, not to foretell the future, but to help us think more intuitively about our situation.

We can make our own oracle. The procedure is very simple.

- Take the Task as Understood

- Generate a random piece of information
- Make connections between the two.

The new piece of information must be generated at random: this is what gives the oracle its power. Random information, being unpredictable, gives us 'a whack on the side of the head', forcing us to look at the problem in a new way.

Finding ways of generating random information can itself be a useful and enjoyable creative exercise. Probably the easiest and least time-consuming method is to use a large dictionary and a pair of dice (refer to 'Making connections' in Chapter 1).

Juxtapose the Task as Understood with the found word. What connections can you make? How can you transform those connections into 'How about's'? Take your time. Go beyond any obvious connection, to a second, third and fourth. Let the juxtaposition spark chains of associations in your mind, and use these as triggers for new ideas. If there seems to be no connection at all, don't give up. There are connections: our task is to find them. The oracle works on the principle that everything is connected to everything else.

Metaphorical thinking

Metaphorical thinking describes or defines something in terms of something else. Analogies show similarities between elements of different things; similes liken one thing to another in a more imaginative way; and metaphors define one thing as another.

We make metaphors continually. We speak of chain reactions and political hot potatoes; we may find ourselves in the depths of despair or all at sea. Metaphorical thinking helps us see reality more vividly. We can use it to find new ideas about a problem.

One of the easiest ways to begin is to examine any metaphor that the client has used in describing the task. Develop the image and ask how you might apply the ideas you discover back in the real world. For example, if a problem with a supplier is that they can't give cast-iron guarantees, we might investigate cast iron: its strengths and weaknesses (withstands heat; tendency to rust); we might ask whether cast iron is the best possible metal for the situation (how about aluminium or gold?); or whether we might do better with an alloy (bronze?). What 'How about's' do these ideas suggest for the Task as Understood?

The analogy game

Pick an action central to the problem. Pick at random one of the actions below and make an analogy by saying: 'This is like that because . . .'

Baking a cake	Running a relay race
Becoming an MP	Dieting
Changing a light-bulb	Looking for fossils
Attending church	Running a day-care centre
Playing Hamlet	Making love
Doing the laundry	Playing Russian roulette
Learning a language	Performing a conjuring trick
Pruning a tree	Getting pregnant
Putting out a fire	Digging for gold
Hunting deer	Swimming the Channel
Applying for a job	Walking across the Sahara
Conducting an orchestra	Planting seeds
Finding a computer virus	Feeding animals at the zoo
Treating an illness	Steering an oil-tanker
Climbing Mont Blanc	Fixing the car

(Make your own list of other activities that you could use as a resource.)

Try to develop the analogy. One connection should lead to another. You needn't make logical sense: puns, jokes, silly images are all useful. If the two activities don't seem to relate, persist. The least obvious analogy may turn out to be the most useful.

Can you correlate elements of the new activity directly to elements in the task?

■ Do the stages of the new activity reflect those of the task?

■ How could improving the way you do one thing suggest improvements or changes in the way you do the task?

Visualization

A picture is worth a thousand words, they say. Yet for many of us, visualizing is a skill we have lost or had educated out of us. Making mental pictures – a kind of structured and willed daydreaming – can suggest many new ideas for solutions if we give it the chance.

Pick a word or picture at random – perhaps using the oracle. Let it trigger a mental picture. Then bring the picture alive and let it take its course, like running a film in your head. Allow it to take whatever twists and turns it wishes. Replay the film after a few minutes and note down the most powerful images or sequences and any ideas that they suggest.

A variation on this technique is to create a 'vision' of your (or the client's) goal – their 'big wish'. Picture the world in which this big wish has come true: what is it like? What is happening? What does it look like? What are the consequences?

Visualization can have powerful side-effects on the team itself. The laughter and enjoyment of making up stories or fantasies can be a strong bonding experience. Minds are opened up and are more flexible than before; people are more cooperative and tolerant; the quality of the listening is greatly improved.

It is vital to maintain a sense of play. Visualization is a powerful psychological process – it is often used as therapy – and it can release material that is difficult to handle. Keep the team focused on the 'game' and encourage a sense of fun.

Identification techniques

We can also visualize by looking at the problem through the eyes of someone – or something – completely different. The trick is to picture yourself in their situation and play out the task.

Imagine you are in a different job: an astronaut, an actor, a soldier, a gardener. How would they tackle the problem? Imagine yourself as:

- A famous figure from history – Julius Caesar, Florence Nightingale, Houdini

- A fictional character – Peter Pan, Anna Karenina, Hamlet, Forrest Gump

- A sports or film star – Meryl Streep, Lynford Christie, Arnold Schwarzenegger.

How would a child deal with the issue? You might hold an internal conversation with someone you respect highly: a mentor or trusted friend. Talk the problem through in your mind and listen to what they tell you. You could even imagine yourself as an animal, insect or plant!

Reversal techniques

These techniques all operate on the principle of turning some aspect of the task inside out, or upside down, or back to front, They involve surfacing and challenging the 'hidden persuaders' that govern our thoughts without our being aware of them. We might call them:

- Rules
- Concepts.

It doesn't really matter what name we give them, as long as we recognize them. We can then challenge them by asking 'What if . . .?' and generate new ideas for tackling the task by transforming each into a 'How about . . .?'

Identify rule/concept >
'What if . . .?' > 'How about . . .?'

It can be difficult to challenge assumptions precisely because we can't see them. It can also feel threatening or frightening to 'think the unthinkable', challenging the very foundations of our thinking. On the other hand, these techniques can produce some of the strongest – and most immediately useful – ideas. They can also be extremely liberating, allowing people to be subversive, to challenge established habits, to think – and utter – the unthinkable.

Remind the team that any reversal is a trigger for new ideas, not an idea for a solution. Concentrate on the idea of reversing, but don't worry about whether the reversal is accurate. Once you've made it, give it time to develop: look for consequences. Don't dismiss any reversal as too outrageous: the crazier, the better.

Rule reversal

What are the rules that govern the Task as Understood? The most obvious might include:

- Laws
- Regulations
- Procedures
- Quality standards.

After some thought, we could add:

- 'Unwritten rules'
- Mottoes and slogans
- Habits
- Morals
- Conventions
- Cultural constraints (community; professional; gender; organizational).

Rules are useful. They help our organizations to run well. They may exist for very sensible operational reasons. But they are temporary, and essentially arbitrary. Our ability to find the potential for new ideas is limited by every rule that we apply. Reverse the rule, and we can release that potential.

Concept challenge

Concepts here are the dominant ideas that define and organize the way we look at things. If we can define them, we can challenge them and liberate our thinking.

We tend to be only vaguely aware of the concepts underlying our thinking. They may govern:

- The organization's vision or mission
- The physical arrangement of the situation

- Our methods or procedures
- The priorities we assign to various elements
- Our reasons for doing something
- The people (or kind of people) we deal with
- The timetable or sequence of events.

Identify the concepts underlying your thinking by writing each one down as a simple sentence: a grammatical sentence of no more than 15 words, containing only one idea. This will help you to define the concept clearly enough for you to challenge it.

Intermediate impossibles

This technique moves in a slightly different direction to achieve reversal. We pick one element of the situation and reverse, distort or exaggerate it. We are looking for the idea that most flouts common sense or received wisdom. This is sometimes called the 'get fired' idea. We then use the intermediate impossible to stimulate a new, feasible solution.

Take only one element at a time. Look for the effects, direct and indirect, of the change you are suggesting. Stay with it: it may take time to see the idea's value. One variant of this technique is to try to work out the most impossible idea. Very few ideas are truly impossible! Try to find one.

Which technique when?

There can be no fixed guidelines for choosing one idea generation technique over another. I've presented the three broad groups of techniques in this chapter roughly in order of 'difficulty'.

1. Using an oracle
2. Metaphorical thinking
3. Reversal techniques

You could introduce them to your brainstorming team in this order. With practice, you will be able to intuit when one technique might be most productive. And, as you and your team become more adept at brainstorming, you will find yourselves creating your own versions of these techniques – or even completely new ones!

Selecting ideas

Having thoroughly enjoyed generating ideas, we now face the tough job of selecting a few to present to the client. They must then choose one to take forward into the final part of the session, where we develop it into a solution that is novel, attractive and feasible.

Decide how many ideas to present for consideration. Experience suggests that half a dozen is probably more than enough at one time. In a 30-minute session, three ideas is probably ample.

The sheer number of ideas we've discovered can be overwhelming. And many of the ideas will be developments or combinations of others, making individual ideas hard to identify.

You may feel that it would be quicker to invite the client to join in the selection process. After all, they will have a better idea of what's novel, attractive and feasible than us! Ask them to concentrate on finding the good ideas rather than weeding out the poor ones. Encourage a 'yes and' approach to each idea chosen, transforming any negative or critical comments into opportunities for building on or improving it.

There are some techniques to help us choose. A combination or sequence of techniques may help to save time.

Intuitive judgement

Otherwise known as 'gut feel'. Using our intuition is particularly useful when the ideas are 'fuzzy' or difficult to quantify.

Although some managers may not like to admit it, intuition plays a large part in many managerial decisions. It can operate very forcibly at this stage in the brainstorming session. The 'obvious' candidates for good solutions may leap out at us with an immediacy and clarity that excites spontaneous approval and pleasure. Check your intuitive response by testing it.

- **Novelty**: is it an idea the client hasn't yet considered?
- **Attractiveness**: is the idea relevant to the client's concerns and priorities?
- **Feasibility**: can we see an immediate, simple and obvious first step?

Intuition can, of course, work strongly against an idea. However feasible it may look 'on paper', something may tell us that it isn't attractive. This can be a useful signal that we need to change the idea in some way: adapt it, combine it with others, break it into parts or take another angle on it.

Intuitive judgement, of course, can also be horribly wrong. But that is no reason to dismiss it. Intuition often speaks to us in a whisper or in code. The danger of not hearing it – or of misreading it – will be lessened if we listen more carefully to it and acknowledge it, rather than simply condemning it as illogical and unbusinesslike.

Clustering

Clustering uses intuition more systematically. It's of special use when we want to understand the relationships between ideas rather than find a single winner.

51

Clustering makes sense of a large number of ideas by grouping them. It will be easier to make choices between the groups than among the individual ideas.

We cluster by writing individual ideas onto Post-its or cards and arranging them into groups on a large table. Look for the connections between ideas, the concepts or themes that link them. Assemble individual ideas around each theme. Some ideas may find their way into more than one category: mark these as particularly strong candidates.

Clustering allows us to think more strategically about our ideas. By grouping them, we lessen the urge simply to accept or reject them. This holds off the final moment of choice and may give us the opportunity to construct an integrated or articulated solution, made up of ideas linked into a larger plan or pattern.

The main risk in clustering is that we group according to preconceived mindsets. The trick is to look for the connections inherent in the ideas we have generated, rather than categorizing them in mental boxes we have already labelled.

Ranking and rating

Ranking places ideas in order of preference; rating scores them against pre-selected criteria. It is a technique we can use when the ideas are similar and clearly comparable.

This quantitative approach scores highly with those who like to put numbers to their judgement. It is the kind of technique often used to select candidates for a job, because it can be an effective corrective to bias, prejudice or 'the halo effect'.

Obviously, this is a far less intuitive technique than clustering; it may therefore seem more attractive to those who distrust gut feel. It may be a more logical way to choose from a group of ideas. But we should remember that ranking and rating are only as rational as our choice of criteria. The technique works most effectively with ideas that are standardized in some way, or a sample from a clearly characterized population: the physical properties of raw materials, for example, or the purely financial criteria for an investment decision.

The first move is to list our selection criteria. We then divide them into 'essentials' and 'desirables'. Desirables are weighted on a scale, say from 1 to 10. Any idea that fails the 'essential' criteria is eliminated. We then rate the remaining ideas against the desirable criteria and add up the scores for each idea. The highest score wins. Easy!

Well, maybe. But the process takes time and may be difficult to perform objectively once you have the ideas in front of you. You might ask the client to establish their 'essentials' and 'desirables' beforehand, but then it would be better for the team not to know them until this point in the brainstorming session: they would otherwise create a powerful constraint on the idea generation process. Ranking and rating can be a useful technique when no one idea captures the team's imagination; on the other hand, a really brilliant new idea creates its own criteria for judgement.

Voting

Voting is a curious mix of intuitive and categorical selection. There is a certain mystique to voting that leads us to assume that it creates fair and reasonable outcomes. It is a powerful ritual suggesting participation, commitment and democracy. Of course, a majority vote for an idea doesn't make it a good one, merely an acceptable one. Voting dresses up intuitive judgement as logical analysis.

Voting can be useful in a number of ways. It can resolve deadlock, when no one idea is self-evidently attractive.

It can lessen the effects of status and power within the team – particularly if it is anonymous. It can also help to sift a large number of ideas and create a sort of consensus by a process of elimination. We might use it to invite each team member to nominate one or more ideas to form a short list. This creates 'sponsors' for ideas and can help the team to select positively. But if we use voting simply to cut short a conflict of views, or to eliminate views that some of the team find uncomfortable, it may lead to rigid behaviour and further discord.

At the end of this part of the session, we have generated many ideas for solutions. We can take only one forward to the last part, where we develop it into a workable plan of action. But many of the others will be matter for more thinking, either as 'fallback solutions' that are more feasible than novel, or as novel possibilities that are not realistic options. Once again, our brainstorming has produced much more material than we can handle immediately: 'by-product' that can be useful on another occasion.

5

DEVELOPING THE SOLUTION

In the last part of the session, we bring back the ideas from our creative excursion and develop them into something of use in the real world (see Figure 7). Our objective is:

- To develop the chosen solution into a practical proposal
- First-stage thinking: the team and client evaluate the idea and explore those aspects that need further development
- Second-stage thinking: we plan the first steps on the road to implementation.

Every new idea, someone has said, is born drowning. So, in order to give our solution the best possible chance, we must build feasibility into it. The more realistically planned it is, the more effectively we'll be able to promote it.

Begin this part of the session by asking the client to explain the chosen solution in their own words. This will ensure that they understand it clearly and sow the seeds of further development. The team then:

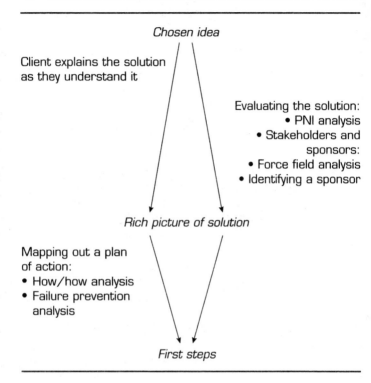

Figure 7 *How to develop the solution*

- Evaluates the solution, transforming potentially negative aspects into new 'How to's' for further creative work
- Maps out a plan of action
- Assesses the possible consequences of the solution
- Identifies the key people who will ensure the solution's success
- Decides on the first steps of the action plan.

The great danger is that nothing will happen. Two of the steps in our plan of action must be:

1. To set a date for following up on what we agree to do
2. To review the success of the brainstorming session itself.

Evaluating the solution

We can evaluate the solution in a number of ways. Our first-stage thinking helps us to see the solution more clearly. The client should first paraphrase the solution as they see it, so that they are certain that they understand it as the team does.

PNI analysis

The easiest way to begin our evaluation is to examine the positive, negative and interesting aspects of our solution, in order. The discipline of attending to each aspect in turn will provide a richer and more detailed picture of the solution.

Looking for what is good about a solution will strengthen it, and give it credibility when it comes to be presented to others (who will be all too ready to criticize or reject it). Looking for its weak features will give us the opportunity to work on them, develop or eliminate them before they see the light of day. By assessing what is interesting about the solution, we begin to reveal its potential impact, and its implications perhaps for other areas of our work.

■ Identify **positive** aspects of the idea: whatever makes it attractive. Don't worry if you can't think of many. Persist: think only about positive features. For each one, ask: 'What further benefits would that bring?' For every benefit, ask: 'How else could we achieve them?' Yet more new ideas may suddenly begin to emerge.

■ Now list the aspects that are **negative** or problematic: weaknesses, shortcomings, risks and dangers. For each one, ask: 'So what is it I need to find?' and try to answer with a 'How to' statement. In this way, a single presented problem can easily turn into half a dozen potential ways of improving the idea.

■ Finally, list the **interesting** aspects of the idea: implications arising from it, the consequences of implementing it, how it will affect other people, potential by-products or spin-offs.

Stakeholders and sponsors

Our solution's success will depend on other people. These include:

■ People who will carry out the actions we've planned

■ Those whose work will be altered by the solution

■ 'Customers' (internal or external) who will see a difference in our products or services

■ Sponsors who can offer support during implementation.

We must take account of all these 'stakeholders'; but we must also be careful not to compromise our own objectives for the sake of 'an easy ride'. When considering the possible consequences of your solution on others, ask:

■ Who would be affected – now and in the future? Short and long term?

■ How will they be affected?

■ What are/will be their views?

■ What effect could those views have on the success of our solution?

■ How could we address those views?

■ Can we prioritize some people for attention?

Identify the 'prime movers' of your plan. In any organization, more people are likely to be involved in implementing a plan than in making it. How will they need to change their behaviour? How soon can you involve them? Have you already involved them by consulting them? What will motivate them to do what you want them to do?

Force field analysis

Any social group – a team, a family, an organization – can be thought of as a system in a state of dynamic equilibrium. A number of forces are operating on and through the people in the system: they are constantly shifting in direction and strength, and the balance between them keeps the system relatively stable. Without the equilibrium between them, the forces in the system would tear it apart.

Implementing a new idea will change the balance of forces and threaten the system's stability. This is one reason why human beings resist being changed: they instinctively understand that change upsets the equilibrium of their social group and hence their sense of security. Pushing in the direction of change will create a pattern of resisting forces as the system tries to regain equilibrium. The system will only change the balance of forces within it if it wants to change.

We will only achieve change within the system if we can remove or lessen the forces resisting change. Force field analysis creates a simple, clear model of the forces supporting and opposing change (see Figure 8).

Analyse systematically. Confine yourself to a specific human system: a single team, department, managerial group or organization. Analyse the forces at work in and on the group – not individuals in the group, or the group conducting the analysis. Consider only the forces you can positively identify, not possible, likely or hypothetical forces.

Present situation ⎯⎯⎯⎯⎯→ Desired situation

Driving forces   Restraining forces

(needs, dissatisfactions,   (economic costs,
shared visions or goals)   fears, anxieties, politics)

Personal
Interpersonal
Group/team/department
Intergroup/team/department
Organizational
Administrative
Technological
Environmental

Figure 8 *Force field analysis*

1. Define the change you want as specifically as possible, as it affects the group ('How to . . .').

2. As driving forces, look for needs within the group, shared dissatisfactions that the change addresses and shared visions of success, goals or targets.

3. As restraining forces, consider: economic costs (which may not be easily quantifiable); psychological costs: fears, anxieties or political opposition to the change, as well as resistance that may result from the change.

4. Address each of the restraining forces by using 'How to' thinking. Draw up plans of actions to lessen or remove each restraining force.

There are a number of general questions to ask in mapping out your action plans.

- What is the relative importance of the forces in the analysis?
- Can we estimate their relative strengths and prioritize them?
- Which forces do we have immediate influence on?
- To whom do we have immediate access?
- How ready is the group for change?
- How can we deal with the psychological costs of change sensitively?
- Where will we have to forge vital links between people to create change?
- What are the consequences on the group of failing to change?

Identifying a sponsor

Many new ideas need sponsorship. To achieve change in an organization requires authority, resources and ability. Wherever all three exist, a sphere of influence develops. Unless we are operating through a sphere of influence, our solution is unlikely to survive.

Spheres of influence may be hard to locate. In traditionally structured organizations, centres of power may be easy to identify – and other spheres of influence may be disguised or hidden. In 'flatter' organizations, all three elements of executive power can be spread between teams, temporary partnerships and autonomous units. Our plan of action then becomes more complicated, involving liaison and networking.

- Who is making all the important decisions in your organization these days?
- What issues are driving the organization at the moment?

- What parts of the organization address those issues most directly?

- How relevant is your plan to those issues?

- What kind of authority would give our solution credibility (financial/technical/marketing/personal)?

The most appropriate sponsor will be the person who can do most to help us implement it. We will recognize them by:

- Their position in the organization

- The size of their budget

- Their authority, explicit and innate

- Their status: their ability to influence others, the value placed on their expertise or opinions and their past record as people who 'make things happen'.

When planning how to approach any sponsor for your idea, concentrate on:

- **Costs**: give an estimate of how much the idea will cost, how much it will save, what the long-term financial benefits are.

- **Help**: how can the sponsor help? Appeal to their role as leader, coach, mentor, trainer.

- **Innovation**: stress the newness of the idea. Any influential decision-maker will want to be associated with new initiatives.

- **Prestige**: what's in it for them?

- **Security**: why is the decision likely to succeed? How well are you managing the risk?

Mapping out a plan of action

It will be easier to believe that our solution will work if we work out the plan of action that will achieve it. It's important not to get embroiled in detail at this point; we must keep our larger objective in view and identify the big steps that will get us there and the resources we will need.

How/how analysis

Begin with the solution and ask 'How do we do that?' Identify a small number of actions. For each of them, ask in turn how they can be achieved. After three or four stages, a number of possible 'chains' of action have been worked out, from broad idea through to specific detail.

A 'how/how' diagram allows us to see alternative courses of action clearly, sift feasible courses of action from implausible ones, identify recurring actions, or detailed actions that will accomplish more than one step and work out a plan of action.

Failure prevention analysis

Failure prevention analysis (FPA) is a systematic technique for estimating what could go wrong with a plan of action. Identifying these risks allows us to plan actions that will minimize them.

FPA involves four steps:

1. Ask: 'What could go wrong?' Identify vulnerable areas of implementation and potential failures.

2. Rank each potential failure by noting its consequences. Estimate:

   – the probability of the failure occurring
   – the seriousness of the consequences.

Rate both probability and seriousness on a scale of one to ten. Multiply both ratings to give an overall rating for each potential failure.

It can be useful to evaluate possible failures according to two distinct criteria:

– consequences for customers
– consequences for the organization.

3. Examine causes of key potential failures. Look for root causes rather than intermediate causes or symptoms.

4. Identify preventative actions. Such actions should aim to eliminate or reduce the root cause of potential failure. They will only reduce the risk of failure: they may not be able to guarantee prevention of failure, but they will help to tip the scales in favour of success.

Taking the first step

The team's final task is to decide on a first step. What will happen, precisely? Record the actions you agree on, allocating names and dates. If people need to coordinate their work, make sure they clearly understand each other's responsibilities and can contact each other easily. Most importantly, make somebody responsible for follow-up.